MW00743715

Reconciliation

A Catechesis for Middle Grades

General Editor
Rev. Gerard P. Weber, S.T.L.

Contributing Editors
Irene H. Murphy
Helen P. Whitaker

Benziger Publishing Company
Woodland Hills, California

Good, Nicholas.
Mrs. Zabel

Illustrations:
Kevin Davidson, Rosanne Litzinger, Norm Merritt, Mike Muir, Linda Sullivan, Susan Staroba, Maryann Thomas

Photography:
Stephen McBrady

Nihil Obstat:
Msgr. Joseph Pollard, S.T.D., V.F.
Censor Deputatus

Imprimatur:
†Roger M. Mahony
Cardinal of Los Angeles
December 6, 1994

The nihil obstat and imprimatur are official declarations that a book or pamphlet is free of doctrinal or moral error. No implication is contained therein that those who have granted the nihil obstat and imprimatur agree with the contents, opinions, or statements expressed.

Scripture passages are taken from the *New American Bible with Revised New Testament.* Revised New Testament of the New American Bible, copyright © 1986 by the Confraternity of Christian Doctrine, Washington, D.C. All rights reserved. Old Testament of the New American Bible, copyright © 1970 by the Confraternity of Christian Doctrine. All rights reserved.

Printed in the United States of America.

Send all inquiries to:
BENZIGER PUBLISHING COMPANY
21600 Oxnard Street, Suite 500
Woodland Hills, California 91367

ISBN 0-02-655931-5

7 8 9 10 11 12 13   073   05 04 03 02 01 00

Contents

1

Welcome

The Greeting

Priest: In the name of the Father, and of the Son, and of the Holy Spirit.

Penitent: Amen.

Priest: May the Lord Jesus welcome you. He came to call sinners, not the just. Have confidence in Him.

Penitent: Amen.

The Chosen One

Moses grew up in the royal palace of the Egyptian Pharaoh, but he never quite fit in. The rest of Pharaoh's grandsons teased and taunted him. "You're adopted!" they told him. "Your mother was an **Israelite** slave!" They even imitated his stutter.

"I'm not adopted!" Moses shouted. "I hate the Israelites!" And to prove so, he beat up one of the Israelite boys who was a palace slave.

Word of the teasing came to Pharaoh's daughter. She called Moses aside. "It's time I told you the truth," she said. "You really are adopted. Your Israelite mother placed you in a basket and put you in the river. She did not want you to be killed or to become a slave. I found you and named you 'Moses,' which means 'drawn out of water.' I took you home and raised you as my own."

From then on, Moses became aware of how cruelly the Egyptians treated the Israelites.

One day, Moses saw an Egyptian whipping an Israelite worker. In anger, Moses killed the Egyptian and buried his body where no one would find him. The next day, Moses saw two Israelite slaves fighting. He decided to run away from Egypt and all of the violence and hatred found there.

Moses went to Midian where he lived safely as a shepherd. He grew up and got married. No one, not even his new bride, knew that he was a murderer.

God Speaks

One day, while Moses was tending sheep, he saw a burning bush. The fire burned and burned, but the leaves of the bush stayed green. Curious, Moses stepped closer. Suddenly, a voice spoke to him from the bush.

"Do not come any closer," the voice said, "for I am God."

Moses thought for sure God would punish him for being a murderer. But instead, God said, "I have seen the suffering of My people in Egypt. I have decided to send you to Pharaoh, so that you can free the Israelites from their slavery."

"But I am a murderer," Moses confessed.

"I know," God replied, "but I want you anyway."

"If I go back to Egypt, Pharaoh will kill me," Moses said.

"I shall be with you," God promised. "No one will harm you."

"I can't do it," Moses argued. "I stutter, and my speech is slow."

"Your brother Aaron speaks well. He can speak for you."

Moses stopped arguing. It was clear that God had chosen him, and not someone else. Although Moses was afraid to return to Egypt, he also felt proud. He was an Israelite, after all, and his people needed him. He knew God loved him in spite of his sin. Maybe he could learn to return that love.

(based on Exodus 2,3,4)

Thinking about Scripture

- Why do you think God chose Moses to lead the Israelites to freedom?
- Why didn't Moses immediately say yes to God?

God's Love

Just about everyone, sooner or later, knows how Moses felt. Perhaps you have felt left out. Maybe you didn't receive an invitation to a friend's party. Maybe you were not chosen to be on a team. Perhaps others have teased you and called you names. Or you might have done something that you felt would keep someone from liking you again.

Being rejected or left out or teased hurts. Jesus knew that because people criticized Him and laughed at Him. They talked about Him and the way He lived and the things He said.

There is Someone who will never reject you or stop loving you. There is Someone who will always make you feel wanted and at home. That Someone is God.

The Call to Love

You don't have to be perfect for God to love you. God loves you right now, the way you are. God's love is so strong that it is bigger than any wrong you might do. No matter what, God keeps on loving you and calling you to become the best person you can be.

This kind of love is hard to believe. And yet there are many stories in the Bible which show how God has loved imperfect people. Moses, who spoke directly to God, was a murderer. Jonah, whom God sent to speak His word, was a coward.

Jesus, too, chose imperfect people to be His friends. The Apostle Peter had a quick temper. James and John often fought with one another. Judas sometimes loved money and power more than he loved people. And Mary Magdalene was so wild that people said she had "seven demons" inside her.

Welcome Home

Just as God welcomed all these people into His Family, so God welcomes you. When your life began, you became the newest member of God's Family. When you received the **sacrament of Baptism,** you became a member of a special part of God's Family—the Catholic Church. The word catholic means "for everyone." Everyone is welcome in the **Catholic Church**. Everyone can belong.

At your baptism, the priest or deacon poured water on you. The water is a sign of new life and new beginnings. As the priest or deacon poured the water, he said, "I baptize you in the name of the Father, and of the Son, and of the Holy Spirit."

These same words are used at the beginning of the sacrament of **Reconciliation**. These words remind you of your baptism. By these words, you say you believe in the **Blessed Trinity**. You want to live as a follower of Jesus.

These words also remind you that God's love is a forgiving love. When you do wrong and feel sorry, God will take you back. God will help you start over. You are called to respond to God's love through the sacrament of Reconciliation. In this sacrament, God says, "Welcome back!"

We Catholics Believe

The Jewish people are called **Israelites** because they are the children of Jacob, whose name was also Israel.

The seven **sacraments** are signs and celebrations of God's power and love. The sacrament of **Baptism** gives new life, washes away sin, and joins us to God's Family.

The members of the **Catholic Church** are baptized and follow the authority of the pope and bishops.

In **Reconciliation,** a person confesses his or her sins to a priest, expresses sorrow for those sins, and promises to do better. The priest forgives the person, in the name of God and the members of God's Family.

Blessed Trinity is our name for the one God who is Father, Son, and Holy Spirit.

Jesus is the Son of God and our Savior.

The Call of Matthew

Matthew went to work each day at the customs post. It was his job to collect taxes from the people and to pay the Roman government. Many people did not trust Matthew, and they disliked him because of his job.

One day, **Jesus** came by the customs post. He saw Matthew sitting there. "Follow Me," Jesus told him.

Matthew didn't know why Jesus was calling him. He only knew that suddenly he felt happy and loved. Leaving everything behind, he got up and followed Jesus.

That night, Matthew gave a big dinner for Jesus at his house. He invited many people, including other tax collectors he knew.

Some people complained about this to Jesus. "Why do you eat and drink with tax collectors and sinners?" they asked Him.

Jesus answered, "Those who are healthy do not need a doctor. Only the sick do. I have not come to call those who are perfect. I have come to call sinners."

From that day, Matthew was one of Jesus' *disciples,* one who believes and follows Jesus. This man that no one had trusted was very glad that Jesus had needed him.

(based on Matthew 9: 9–13)

Thinking about Scripture

- What made Matthew want to follow Jesus?
- What is one way you are needed by Jesus?

A Forgiveness Story

The followers of Jesus had faults, yet Jesus forgave them and challenged them to live the way He did.

You can do the same. Use the boxes to draw a picture-story about a time someone hurt you or made you angry. Let the final drawing show you forgiving the person in words or actions.

Vocabulary

Write your own definitions for the following words:

Catholic _a religion of the world._

Reconciliation _a sacrament that brings you closer to God._

Signs of God's Love

God shows His love for you and for your family in many ways. God has created a wonderful world for you to live in. God has given you life and people who care about you. God has given you many gifts and talents.

Find a time when the members of your family can meet. Then, work together to fill the frame below with words or pictures that are signs of God's love for your family.

love   health   happiness

forgiveness

considerate

giving

innerpeace

kindness bonding

togetherness

peace

Finally, say this prayer together:

Heavenly Father, we see Your love in our home and in the ways we show we care. You are present when we smile at one another and when we take the time to listen. We feel Your presence when we forgive and when we show that our love will never end. Help us make this love grow. Amen.

Family Note: Lesson 1 opens with the Greeting that begins the sacrament of Reconciliation. The purpose of the lesson is to explain that God always loves us, inspite of our faults, and shows us love in many ways.

Rules of Love

The Word of God

Priest: Come to Me, all you that labor and are heavily burdened, and I will give you rest.

Penitent: Glory and praise to You, Lord Jesus Christ.

Priest: The Lord be with you.

Penitent: And also with you.

Priest: A reading from the holy Gospel according to Matthew (or Mark, or Luke, or John).

Penitent: Glory to You, Lord.

Loving

Moses and Aaron were able to do what God had called them to do. They led the Israelites safely away from Egypt. They freed the people from their slavery.

At first, the Israelites were happy. But soon, they did not know what to do with their new freedom. They began to fight and argue among themselves. They stole one another's food and clothing, and they lied and cheated. Children disobeyed their parents. Old people were left to die. It seemed that no one loved anyone else any more.

"Our lives are miserable," the people complained to Moses. "You should have left us in Egypt."

Moses didn't know what to say. But he knew that God would have an answer. After all, God had promised to be with them.

Rules of Love

So Moses climbed Mount Sinai to pray. "The people need to know You love them," Moses said to God. "Please give them some sign that You care."

Moses prayed for three days. On the third day, there was a clap of thunder. Lightning flashed across the sky, and the whole mountain shook. Finally, God spoke.

"I am the Lord, your God, who brought you out of Egypt. You shall have no gods but Me.

You shall not use My name in vain.

Remember the Sabbath and keep it holy.

Honor your father and mother.

You shall not kill.

You shall not commit adultery.

You shall not steal.

You shall not lie.

You shall not desire your neighbor's wife.

You shall not desire anything that belongs to your neighbor."

Then, Moses was told that these **Ten Commandments** were a sign of His love. "Tell the people how much I love them," God said. "Let them know that I want the best for them. If they truly love Me, they will follow My commandments."

Moses brought the Ten Commandments back to the people. And wherever the people traveled, they carried God's rules with them. They knew they had been chosen to be loved by God, and to show their love in return.

(based on Exodus 16, 20)

Thinking about Scripture

- What problems did the Israelites have in dealing with their freedom?
- How can rules be a sign of love?

The Ten Commandments

On Mount Sinai, God made a **covenant** with the Israelites. God's part of the covenant was to show saving love at all times. The people's part of the agreement was to respond in love to God and to one another.

When people love you very much, they see the good in you. They see what is possible for you. And when you know you are loved, you want to be the best you can be. This is how it was to be between God and the Israelites.

The Ten Commandments showed the Israelites what God expected of them. The commandments also were a sign of God's presence with them. When Moses brought the Law down from the mountain, the Israelites looked upon it as their most precious possession.

Growing in Love

The covenant God made with the Israelites is our covenant, too. We show responsibility and gratitude for God's promise of saving love when we follow the commandments.

We grow in our love for God and for others whenever we follow the Ten Commandments. The first three commandments tell what is expected of us in our relationship with God. The last seven commandments tell what is expected of us in our relationship with ourselves and with others.

Throughout our lives, we grow in our understanding of the Ten Commandments. Read through the commmandments. Think about what they say to you at the age you are now and what they'll mean to you as you grow older.

Commandment	What It Means
I am the Lord, your God. You shall have no other gods besides me.	Think about God and talk to God often. Tell others about your faith.
You shall not take God's name in vain.	Use God's name and Jesus' name with respect. Do not use God's name in anger or make fun of any holy person, place, or thing.
Keep holy the Sabbath.	Celebrate Sunday with the Eucharist, joy, thanksgiving, and rest.
Honor your father and mother.	Obey and respect your parents. Be kind to all older people.
You shall not kill.	Respect and care for all living things.
You shall not commit adultery.	Respect your body and the bodies of others. Be modest in the way you dress and act.
You shall not steal.	Do not take things from others. Do not cheat.
You shall not lie.	Tell the truth. Do not gossip about others.
You shall not desire your neighbor's wife.	Remember that marriage is holy. Show respect for family life.
You shall not desire anything that belongs to your neighbor.	Do not be jealous of what others have. Be a good sport and a good loser. Do not waste money on things you do not need.

We Catholics Believe

A **covenant** is a solemn agreement between two people or nations. God's covenant with the Israelites was a sacred and loving agreement. God promised to be with them always; the Israelites promised to follow the Ten Commandments. God's covenant is different from ordinary covenants, because it is based on complete love and respect. It also lasts forever.

The **Great Commandment** is the name given to the words of Jesus that tell us to love God and our neighbor.

The Command to Love

In the days of Jesus, there were many teachers who spent all their time studying God's Word and God's Law. People took their covenant with God very seriously.

One day, some people decided to ask Jesus to settle a question for them. They wanted to test Jesus' knowledge of the Scriptures. We call His answer the **Great Commandment** because it sums up all of God's rules of love.

"Teacher," they asked Him, "which commandment is the greatest?"

Jesus answered, "You know the commandment your ancestors taught you: 'You shall love the Lord, your God with all your heart, with all your soul, with all your strength, and with all your mind.'" Jesus added another line. "You shall love your neighbor as yourself."

The people were amazed. Not only had Jesus answered correctly, He had also given them an answer no one could argue with!

Later, on the night before He died, Jesus talked to His disciples in private. He explained more about what God expected of them. "I give you a new commandment," Jesus told them. "Love one another as I have loved you. This is how people will know that you are My disciples, if you have love for one another."

(*based on Mark 12:28–34 and John 15:9–17*)

Thinking about Scripture

- Say the Great Commandment in your own words.
- Why do you think love is such an important part of God's Law?

Keeping the Rules

Each commandment tells a good way to live.
Draw a line that connects the commandment to
the action it tells to do.

Commandment	What to Do
I am the Lord your God...	Admit to the wrong you did.
Honor your father and mother.	Pay for what you want in a store.
You shall not steal.	Do your chores without being told.
You shall not kill.	Pray and love God.
You shall not lie.	Eat healthy foods.

Each commandment also tells what *not* to do.
Draw a line that connects the commandment and
the action it says to avoid.

Commandment	What Not to Do
Keep holy the Sabbath.	Fight with your brothers and sisters.
Honor your father and mother.	Be jealous of something your friend has.
You shall not want your neighbor's goods.	Pretend not to hear your mom when she needs you.
You shall not take God's name in vain.	Miss Mass on Sunday because you feel lazy.
You shall not kill.	Use Jesus' name when you are angry.

Vocabulary

Write your own definitions for the following words:

Covenant _An agreement between someone and ?_

Word of God _The law of God._

We Pray to the Holy Family

Leader: We gather in the name of the Father, and of the Son, and of the Holy Spirit.

All: Amen.

Leader: Jesus, You loved Your parents and You learned from them.

All: Jesus, Mary, and Joseph, teach us how to show respect. Help us listen to one another and to live what we learn.

Leader: Hail Mary, full of grace! You said yes and became the Mother of God. You showed Jesus how to care for others.

All: Jesus, Mary, and Joseph, teach us how to obey. Help us see when someone needs us. Help us say yes.

Leader: Saint Joseph, you were like a father to Jesus. You gave Him a home, shared your faith, and showed Jesus a trade.

All: Jesus, Mary, and Joseph, teach us to love. Help us learn new things, share what we know, and do the best we can, in whatever we're doing.

Leader: Holy Family, may our actions bring us closer to our heavenly Creator and to one another. Amen.

Family Note: Lesson 2 opened with the second step in the sacrament of Reconciliation: listening to Scripture. It continued into an explanation of the Ten Commandments as signs of God's faithfulness and love. Jesus gave us a new commandment that we call the Great Commandment. Talk about all of these commandments with your child and how they relate to everyday living.

3 Right and Wrong

Examination of Conscience

Leader: God, our Father, sometimes we have not behaved as Your children should.

Penitents: But You love us and come to us.

Leader: We have given trouble to our parents and teachers.

Penitents: But You love us and come to us.

Leader: We have quarreled and called each other names.

Penitents: But You love us and come to us.

Leader: We have been lazy at home and in school, and have not been helpful to our parents (brothers, sisters, friends).

Penitents: But You love us and come to us.

Leader: We have thought too much of ourselves and have told lies.

Penitents: But You love us and come to us.

Leader: We have not done good to others when we had the chance.

Penitents: But You love us and come to us.

Obeying

In the beginning, God created the heavens and the earth and all that live within them. Then, God created Adam, the first man, and Eve, the first woman. They were created with an understanding heart, wisdom, and knowledge. God loved Adam and Eve very much and gave them a beautiful garden in which to live.

The garden was lush with all kinds of trees and herbs and bushes and flowers. And in the middle of the garden, God planted a special tree. It was a tall, beautiful tree. God called it the Tree of Knowledge.

"You can eat as much as you want from every tree in this garden," God told Adam and Eve. "But you may not touch the Tree of Knowledge. If you eat from that tree, you will know about good and evil. You will know suffering and pain. One day, you will die."

Adam and Eve did as God told them and lived in peace.

The First Sin

Now the Tempter was jealous of Adam and Eve's happiness. So the Tempter came to Eve in the form of a serpent.

"Aren't you hungry?" the serpent asked her. "Why don't you try some of this fruit? It looks sweet and juicy."

"No," said Eve. "If I eat that fruit, God said I will die."

The serpent laughed. "You won't die. You'll just get smart. Once you eat the fruit of this tree, you'll know as much as God."

Eve was hungry. The serpent's words seemed to make sense. She knew she was breaking her promise to God, but she took some fruit from the tree and ate it. It was delicious! Eve thought Adam would like it, and so she gave him some to eat, too.

Just then, God called out to Adam and Eve.

Suddenly, they felt cold and afraid. They knew they had done wrong. From then on, Adam and Eve would no longer be so understanding and wise. They would

feel a pull toward evil, as well as good. They would no longer be able to live in the garden. And someday they would die.

(*based on Genesis 2,3*)

Thinking about Scripture

- Why did Adam and Eve disobey God?
- What does the story about Adam and Eve tell about the way sin entered the world?

Right and Wrong Choices

The members of God's Family have a special reason for telling the story of Adam and Eve. We are all children of those first parents, and so the results of that first sin are with us. Every human being feels a pull between choosing what is right and choosing what is wrong. Every person can make wrong choices and turn away from God.

We call the choice of the first people to turn away from God **original sin**. Jesus saved us from original sin but its effects—sin, misery, and evil—are still with us. In Baptism, we receive God's **grace**—God's life and love—to overcome sin and evil. But it does not work by magic. We have the gift of **free will**. Throughout our lives, we always have a choice.

Sin and Forgiveness

Like Adam and Eve, we can choose to obey God's Commandments, or we can choose to disobey them. Sin is choosing to do wrong. It means turning away from God. **Sin** hurts the sinner and sin hurts others, too.

Nothing can hurt God, but sin hurts our friendship with God. *Venial sin* weakens our friendship. *Mortal sin* is very serious, because it ruins our friendship with God. Mortal sin is sometimes called "deadly sin," because it separates us from grace, our share in God's life.

Every sin involves a choice. A sin is mortal when the action is seriously wrong, the person knows the action is seriously wrong, and chooses to commit the action anyway. No one can commit a mortal sin by mistake or by accident.

Nothing, not even sin, can make God stop loving us. How we answer that love is our choice. When we say yes to that love, we grow in holiness. When we say no, even then, God's love is strong and pulls us to good.

Pulling Us to Good

God gives us a special gift to help us know how to use the freedom to choose. It's called **conscience**. Conscience is the ability we have to say, "This is a good choice," or "That is a sin." It's not something that goes off automatically, like an alarm clock. We need to work with our conscience and to practice using it wisely. Prayer, study, and the sacraments are ways to form our conscience and keep it on the right track.

Jesus gave us the sacrament of Reconciliation to help us make peace with God and with God's Family. One step in the sacrament of Reconciliation is an *examination of conscience*. This involves taking a close and honest look at the choices made and the actions taken. We ask ourselves: Which were good choices? Which were against God's Law? What are some reasons I made the choices I did? How did these choices affect me? affect others? How can I make better choices in the future?

We Catholics Believe

Original sin is the first sin. Only Jesus and His Mother, Mary, were born without original sin. Baptism frees us from original sin, but its effects are still with us.

In Baptism, we receive **grace,** a share in God's life and love, to overcome sin and evil.

God's gift of **free will** allows us to choose to walk with Jesus or to walk away from God.

Sin is forgiven in the sacrament of Reconciliation.

The **conscience** is the ability to know right from wrong. This gift is developed by listening to the teachings of the Church, and by praying, studying, and participating in the sacraments.

The Two Sons

Jesus told many special stories, or *parables*, as a way of teaching. One day, He told His friends this story.

There was a vineyard owner who had two sons. Since it was harvest time, the man needed extra help in his vineyard. So he went to his first son. "I really need your help today," he said. "Please come with me to the vineyard."

The first son shook his head. "I can't work for you today," he answered. "I already made plans with my friends."

Disappointed, the man went to his second son. "I need your help with the grapes today," he said.

"I'll be right there," the boy answered.

The man went to the field, expecting his second son to follow. But the second son changed his mind. "I know I told my father I would help him," he thought. "But it's hot today, and I'd much rather go swimming." So he went swimming, and never went to the field.

Meanwhile, the first son was on his way to meet his friends. He thought to himself, "My father is always very good to me. I made him sad today when I said I wouldn't help him. I can always play with my friends another day." So the boy hurried to the vineyard to help his father.

Jesus looked at His friends. "Which one of these boys obeyed his father?"

(based on Matthew 21:28–31)

Thinking about Scripture

- How would you answer Jesus' question?

Obeying God's Law

We can live our faith by knowing our beliefs. Fill in the blanks to make the sentences complete.

1. Sin is choosing to do _wrong_ .

2. We suffer from sin, pain, and misery, which are the results of the first sin, called _original_ sin.

3. _Mortal_ sin is sometimes called deadly sin.

4. God gave you a _free will_ to help you know right from wrong.

5. For a sin to be mortal, it is necessary that:

   a. The action is _seriously_ wrong.

   b. The person _knows_ it is _seriously_ wrong.

   c. The person freely _chooses_ to do the wrong.

6. _Grace_ , which is God's life and love within us, helps us overcome sin and evil.

7. Sin is forgiven in the sacrament of _Reconciliation_ .

8. An _examination_ of _conscience_ helps us look at the choices we made.

Vocabulary

Give an example of each:

Venial sin _lie_

Mortal sin _killing_

Parable _a special story like ?_

Grace-Filled Lives

One way to pray is to ask yourself questions. Then, give yourself time to think about the answers. Try that with this prayer:

Leader: People have always asked, "Who am I?" King David asked this question in this way:

All: A reading from Psalm 8:

O Lord, I behold Your heavens, and the work of Your fingers, the moon and stars which You set in place. Who am I that You should care for me?

Leader: Let us be quiet and reflect. Think about who you are right now. (Pause briefly after each question.) What makes you happy? What are some of your worries? What is important to you? Think about the future. What would you like to be doing ten or fifteen years from now? You have been made in God's image. That means you are good. Spend a little time thinking about the goodness inside of you. (Pause).

All: God, our Creator, thank You for your gift of grace. May this sharing of Your life help us as we try to follow Jesus to Your kingdom. Amen.

I Confess

Confession

Penitent: I confess to almighty God, and to you, my brothers and sisters, that I have sinned through my own fault in my thoughts and in my words, in what I have done, and in what I have failed to do; I ask blessed Mary, ever virgin, all the angels and saints, and you, my brothers and sisters, to pray for me to the Lord our God.

Confessing

Tom was Patty's next-door neighbor and good friend. One day, Tom saw Patty sitting on the step of her porch. She looked very sad.

"What's the matter?" Tom asked as he sat next to Patty.

Patty sighed. "I'm in trouble with everyone," she confessed.

"Like who?" Tom asked.

"My mom and dad for one thing," Patty answered. "I lied to them last night. I said my grades in school were good. I told them I didn't need to study. So my mom and dad let me watch television. Today, they saw my report card. It's really bad. Now I can't watch television for two weeks."

"I can see why you're sad," said Tom.

"Yeah," said Patty, "but that's not the end of it. This morning, I was playing with my mom's hair dryer. I dropped it and cracked the handle. Now the dryer won't work."

When's It Going to End?

"Does your mom know?" asked Tom.

Patty shook her head. "I've been afraid to tell her. She's already mad at me about my grades. Besides, just now, when I went to get something to drink, I spilled a whole gallon of punch all over the inside of the refrigerator. Mom's still trying to clean the sticky mess."

Tom frowned. "You're sure having a bad day!"

Patty nodded in agreement. "I found Chrissy fooling around with my stamp collection. I yelled at her, and I pulled her hair. She cried and ran to dad. And he blamed me for being mean. Now I feel just rotten."

Tom and Patty were quiet for a moment.

Then Tom said, "Patty, I think you should look back over what happened today. Some of the trouble was your fault. You should work that out with your folks. But some of the stuff was an accident. You can forget about that."

Patty started to smile. "You're right!" She headed back in the house. "Thanks," she said. "It sure helps to talk."

Thinking about the Story

- Which actions were Patty's fault? Which were accidents?
- How did Tom help Patty?

Responsibility

The word **responsible** comes from the same root as "respond." It means "to answer." Being responsible means knowing that there is a difference between right and wrong. It means being answerable for your choices and accepting the consequences.

Every choice or action has **consequences**—things that follow naturally from that choice or action. These consequences may help or hurt you, and they may help or hurt others. Being responsible means choosing actions that will have the best possible consequences, not only for you but for others.

Accident, Mistake, or Sin?

Sometimes, people confuse accidents or mistakes with sin. An *accident* is something that happens without your control. You do not choose to have an accident. Patty did not think: "Gee, I'd like to spill this punch all over the refrigerator."

A *mistake* involves an incorrect choice. You may think you know the right answers to your history test, but you may be incorrect. Mistakes are choices that you make without the right information.

Sin is a choice that you know is wrong, but you make anyway. Patty knew that her grades were bad, but she chose to lie to her parents so that she could watch television. Patty's lie was a sin.

Knowing the difference among accidents, mistakes, and sin is something we all need to know. But that's just the first step. Next comes figuring out how to take responsibility for our actions. Patty realized that she would need to take responsibility in different ways for lying and for hurting her sister, than for the spilling of the punch and the dropping of the hair dryer.

Confession

Jesus wants us to grow in personal responsibility. That is why He has gave us a special gift, to help everyone show sorrow for wrong choices and to learn to make better choices. This gift is the sacrament of Reconciliation.

In the sacrament of Reconciliation, you confess your sins to the priest. You admit that you have made wrong choices. This **confession** is usually a conversation. The priest may ask you questions. The priest may help you decide which actions were really sins and which ones were accidents or mistakes. Then the priest may suggest ways for you make better choices in the future.

This part of the sacrament is a lot like Patty's conversation with Tom. The priest is not there to yell at you or to make you feel sad. He is doing for you what Jesus did for His friends—listening, asking questions, and helping you make peace with God. You do not have to be afraid to talk to the priest about anything that is bothering you. Your conversation is private.

In the sacrament of Reconciliation, you accept the blame for your wrong actions. You say that you are sorry and that you are going to do better. These are very important steps in developing a sense of responsibility.

We Catholics Believe

Being **responsible** means to be answerable for the choices you make.

A **consequence** is something that results from a choice or action. The consequences of sin include separation from God and from God's Family. In the case of mortal sin, a person may not receive Jesus in Holy Communion until the sin has been confessed and forgiven in the sacrament of Reconciliation. We believe that a person who dies refusing to ask forgiveness for mortal sin will be separated from God's love forever. The name for this separation is **hell**.

Confession is the act of telling your sins to the priest in the sacrament of Reconciliation.

Messiah is a name for the Savior promised by God. Jesus is the Messiah.

The Good Thief

After Jesus was sentenced to die, the soldiers took Him to a place that was nicknamed "the Skull." They crucified Him there, along with two other criminals. One of these criminals was on His right, and the other was on His left.

One of the criminals hanging there was mean to Jesus. "I thought You were the **Messiah,** the One chosen by God to save us," he said. "If so, why don't You save Yourself and us, too?"

The other criminal, however, said to the first criminal, "You have no right to speak to Jesus like that. You and I deserve this punishment. We committed bad crimes. But Jesus does not deserve this. He has done nothing wrong."

Then this criminal said to Jesus, "Remember me, Lord, when You come into Your kingdom."

Jesus knew that the criminal was sorry for his sins. So Jesus said to him, "Amen, I say to you, today you will be with Me in heaven."

(*based on Luke 23:33–43*)

Thinking about Scripture

- Why do you think Jesus forgave the second thief?

Making Choices

Decide whether each example below is an accident, a mistake, or a sin. On the lines, write an **A** if it is an accident, an **M** if it is a mistake, or an **S** if it is a sin.

A 1. Your marker slips out of your fingers when you are drawing, and you make a mark on the table.

S 2. You hit your brother because he is playing in your room.

M 3. You set your alarm clock for 8:30 instead of 7:30, forgetting that you have an early soccer game.

S 4. Your Mom asks you to take out the trash, but you pretend you didn't hear her.

A 5. While wrestling in fun with a friend, you both fall, and he breaks an arm.

S 6. You want money for ice cream. You take some from your sister's wallet without asking her.

M 7. You take the wrong bus, and you are late for your dentist appointment.

A 8. You lean over, and your glasses fall off and break.

good

Vocabulary

Write your own definitions for the following words:

Confess _say you're sorry for what you did_

Consequence _a price you have to pay_

Responsibility _something you have to do yourself_

✓ *good consequences can come from good actions.*

Making Choices

Leader: We gather together to pray in the name of the Father, and of the Son, and of the Holy Spirit.

All: Amen.

Leader: In one of his letters, Saint Paul wrote: "Sometimes, I cannot understand why I do what I do. Instead of doing what I love, I do what I hate. Instead of doing what I know what is right, I do what is wrong" (*based on Romans 7:15–20*). We have all felt this way. Let us ask God to help us choose wisely, especially when this is difficult to do.

Reader 1: Sometimes it's hard to do what is right when my friends want me to do otherwise.

All: Lord, our God, call us out of darkness into light.

Reader 2: There are temptations to do wrong when I know I can get away with it.

All: Lord, fill our hearts with courage.

Reader 3: There are many mixed messages in the world about what is right and what is wrong.

All: Jesus, let us look to Your teachings for answers.

Leader: Let us join together and say,

All: O God, You know everything—when we make good choices and when we sin. Help us be more responsible in the way we follow Your commandments. Before we act, let us consider how our actions will help or hurt others. Be with us. Amen.

Family Note: Lesson 4 focuses on the importance of confession, in everyday life and in the sacrament of Reconciliation. In our daily living, we are expected to take responsibility for our choices, and to consider the consequences of our actions before we make a choice. In the sacrament, we confess our sinful choices and offer to take responsibility to be better.

5 Being Sorry

Act of Contrition

Priest: Now, with Jesus, our Brother, we come before our Father in heaven and ask Him to forgive our sins.

Penitent: My God, I am sorry for my sins with all my heart. In choosing to do wrong and failing to do good, I have sinned against You, whom I should love above all things. I firmly intend, with Your help, to do penance, to sin no more, and to avoid whatever leads me to sin. Our Savior Jesus Christ suffered and died for us. In His name, my God, have mercy.

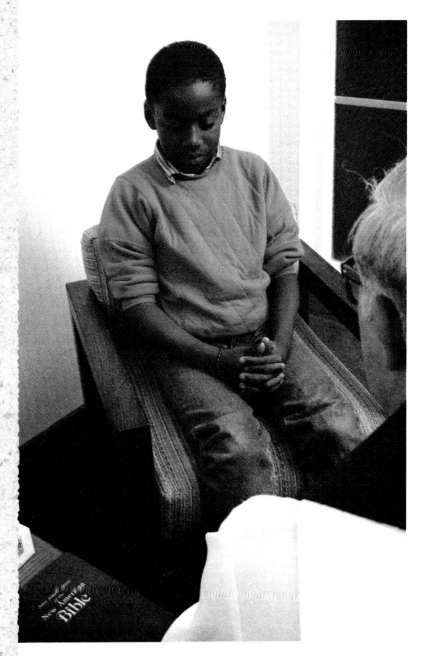

Making Peace

Joe loved to play baseball. He played at school and on an after-school team. He also played at home, even though there wasn't a lot of room in his backyard. Joe had been told over and over again not to play in the yard. But he did anyway.

One day, Joe's friend Eddie pitched him a perfect ball. Joe felt the bat meet the ball. He heard the crack. He saw the ball lift and sail out—a home run! The ball kept flying, over Joe's back fence. And then, with an awful crash, it smashed into the Mitchells' living-room window.

The excitement vanished, and Joe felt terrible. He knew right away that he had done something wrong.

Mr. and Mrs. Mitchell were really angry, and called Joe's parents to complain. "There's glass all over the living room!" Mr. Mitchell said. "And our cat jumped out through the broken window and ran away!"

Making Good Again

Joe sat down with his parents. He felt like crying. "What can I do to get out of this?" Joe asked.

"You need to make peace with the Mitchells," Joe's dad answered.

"I really am sorry," Joe said.

"Show the Mitchells that you're sorry," Joe's mom added.

"How do I do that?" Joe asked.

"You can tell them you'll be more careful in the future," his mom said. "You can keep your promise not to play baseball in the yard."

"There's still the broken window," Joe's dad said.

"And the cat," Joe added, sighing. "I guess I should try to make up for the damage I did. Making peace is hard work!"

"Sometimes it is," his dad agreed. "But we've all had to do it at one time or another."

Joe took his parents' advice. He went out right away and looked around the yard. He found the Mitchells' cat curled up under the Barkleys' car. Joe coaxed the cat into his arms and walked nervously over to the Mitchells' house.

"I'm really sorry," Joe told Mr. and Mrs. Mitchell. "I promise it won't happen again. And I'll save the money I get for my paper route to pay for a new window."

Mr. and Mrs. Mitchell understood. They told Joe that they forgave him. Mr. Mitchell even offered to help Joe with his batting practice—at the park!

Thinking about the Story

- Why was the broken window not an accident?
- What did Joe do to make peace with the Mitchells?

Asking for Forgiveness

Sin is a kind of selfishness. When we are selfish, we think only about ourselves. We know what we want, and we want it right now. We don't think about how our actions may hurt us, or hurt others. Or, we simply don't care.

Joe was being selfish when he disobeyed his parents and played baseball in the yard. He didn't think about what would happen if he disobeyed. He didn't wonder how his actions might affect his neighbors.

Every time we choose sin, we become less sensitive—less aware and caring—of others. We build a kind of wall of selfishness between ourselves and others, and between ourselves and God's love. That wall disturbs the peace. That is what Joe learned.

Disturbing the Peace

The word peace has many meanings. There is the type of inner peace that comes when a person feels a sense of well-being or security. There is another type of peace in which two enemies settle their conflicts without using any weapons. There is a third type of peace that results when a person has a good relationship with God.

Sin hurts all these kinds of peace. **Forgiveness** is the way to make peace again. Forgiveness begins with the desire to be forgiven. It has to be asked for. That's why saying "I am sorry" is so important. To say "I'm sorry" is to say "I was wrong. Please forgive me." It also means "I really do care. I want us to be at peace again."

To admit to being wrong takes a certain amount of **humility**—the ability to be honest. Being humble is not always easy. That is why Jesus helps the members of God's Family through the sacrament of Reconciliation.

Making Peace

In the sacrament of Reconciliation, the priest, who stands for Jesus and for the Christian **community**, welcomes you with kindness. He shares a story of God's forgiveness from the Bible. Then, you talk to the priest about the sins you have committed. You say that you are sorry for your sins. Before God and before the priest, you say "I am sorry" in an **Act of Contrition**. You promise to try not to sin again. Once you have said "I am sorry," you are on your way to being forgiven.

Learning to be thoughtful of others is a way to keep the promise to be better. Jesus shows us how in these words: "Do to others whatever you would have them do to you." We call this way of living the **Golden Rule**.

Forgiveness is the act of pardoning someone who hurt you.

Humility is the ability to be honest about yourself and to accept your good points and bad points. Humble people can admit when they are wrong. They have the courage to say "I'm sorry."

A group of people who share something in common is called a **community**. The Church is a community because its members believe in and follow Jesus.

Contrition is sorrow for sin and the promise to do better. In the sacrament of Reconciliation, you say you are sorry by praying an **Act of Contrition**.

Around two hundred years age, people gave the **Golden Rule** its name because it is so precious.

Peter's Denial

On the night before He died, Jesus ate supper with His friends. "Tonight, your faith in Me will be shaken," He told them.

Peter refused to believe it. "Mine will never be," he claimed.

But Jesus knew better. "I say to you, this very night before the rooster crows, you will deny Me three times."

"Lord," Peter protested, "you know I would rather die than deny You!"

That night, soldiers arrested Jesus and took him to the court of the high priest. Peter was very afraid, but he followed them to the courtyard.

He was sitting by the fire when one of the maids came over to him. "You were with Jesus," she said to him.

"I don't know what you are talking about!" Peter answered.

Another girl recognized him. "You were with Jesus," she said.

Again Peter denied it. "I do not even know the man," he lied.

A little later, a crowd of people came over and said to Peter, "Surely, you are one of the followers of Jesus. You even talk like His friends."

Peter began to curse and swear. "I do not know the man!" he insisted.

Just then, a rooster began to crow. And Peter remembered the words Jesus had spoken. Peter was very sorry for what he had done. He went out of the courtyard and began to cry. In his heart, he asked Jesus to forgive him.

(*based on John 18:15–18, 25–27*)

Thinking about Scripture

• Why do you think Peter pretended he didn't know Jesus?

Peace Puzzle

There are many words that have to do with repentance. Complete each sentence with the correct word. Write the word in the numbered spaces. What message do you read in the boxes?

1. When we _sin_, we hurt the peace between ourselves and God, and between ourselves and others.

2. Mr. and Mrs. Mitchell were _angry_ because Joe broke their window.

3. Joe needed to _make peace_ with Mr. and Mrs. Mitchell.

4. We are _selfish_ when we think only about ourselves, and not about others.

5. _contrition_ is the attitude of being sorry for sin.

6. "Do to others whatever you would have them do to you" is the Golden _rule_.

7. "I am sorry" is a way to ask someone to _forgive_ you for what you did wrong.

8. "I am sorry" also means "I will _try_ to do better."

Vocabulary

Write your own definitions for the following words:

Peace _niceness; happiness, and joy_

Humility _being meek + being honest about yourself._

43

Showing Contrition

Find a time when the members of your family can meet together. Then ask each person to write or tell answers to the following questions:

What was one time when I was not
at peace with another family member?

What happened to restore the peace?

What is one way I have been forgiven?

Then, in the space below, write your own Family Act of Contrition. Ask God to help you forgive one another. You can pray your prayer together.

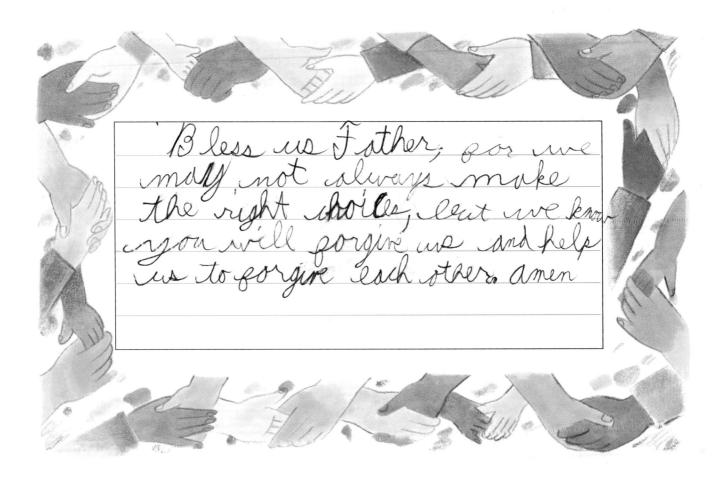

Bless us Father, for we may not always make the right choice, but we know you will forgive us and help us to forgive each other. amen

Family Note: Lesson 5 stresses contrition as an important part of the sacrament of Reconciliation, as well as a necessary part of everyday living. Help your child see the importance of being sorry for wrong choices. Model forgiveness in your home. To write the Family Act of Contrition, you may wish to refer to the prayers found on page 78.

6 Changing Your Life

Receiving A Penance

Priest: Have you confessed all your sins?

Penitent: Yes.

Priest: Will you try to change what you were doing wrong?

Penitent: Yes.

Priest: For your penance, then, I ask that you say a prayer (or do something to make up for your wrong choices). This will help you to make peace and to grow as a follower of Jesus.

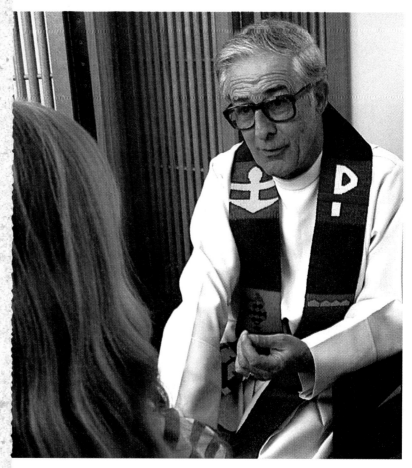

Changing

Jody Phillips had a problem. Every time she got angry, she would yell at her younger sister, Anne. Sometimes, she would even hit Anne.

Mrs. Phillips didn't like the situation. One day, Mrs. Phillips sent Jody to her room. "Stay there," Jody's mom said, "until you're ready to live in peace with Anne."

"Mom," Jody asked, "can't I just say I'm sorry to Anne?"

"Saying you're sorry is the first step," her mother replied. "If you say you're sorry now, and then tomorrow you start yelling and hitting again, you haven't changed anything. I think you need some time out to come up with a better way to treat your sister."

Jody sat staring out the window. She thought about what her mother had said. It would be a lot easier just to tell Anne she was sorry. Changing was hard.

The Next Step

Jody got a sheet of paper and a pencil from her desk. She thought for a long time. Then, she made a list of all the things she could do when she got angry. And even though she knew it would be difficult, Jody left yelling and hitting off her list.

Mrs. Phillips smiled and gave her a hug when Jody showed her the list. "This is a good start," she said. "We'll all try to help you."

Jody told Anne she was sorry. She promised to try very hard not to take her anger out on Anne. Jody even played a game with Anne, without quarreling.

The next day, Jody came home from school in a bad mood. Her bus was late. She had extra homework. And then she saw that someone had taken the last chocolate chip cookie from the jar. Jody ran to her room and slammed her books down.

Anne was waiting. She had game pieces spread out all over Jody's room. And she had the last cookie in her hand. Anne took one look at Jody's angry face, and then, she ran.

Without thinking, Jody started to yell. She turned to run after Anne. Then, Jody's eyes fell on the list she had made. She took a deep breath. She took a pillow from her bed and began to punch it over and over.

Soon, she began to feel silly, and started to laugh. Jody wasn't angry any more. She even felt proud that she had begun to change her ways.

"Anne," Jody called. "I've got time for one quick game."

"I saved you half a cookie," Anne said, coming back. Jody laughed and hugged her little sister. Changing wasn't easy—but for now, it felt very good.

Thinking about the Story

- Why did Jody have to do more than just say she was sorry?
- How did Jody prove she was really sorry for what she had done to Anne?

Conversion

Jesus began His teaching with this message: "Reform your lives. Turn away from sin. Try to be better." This is a message that members of God's Family still need to hear. It is a message of change, a message of **conversion.** Whenever we choose to do wrong, we need to change, or reform, our lives. Like Jody Phillips, we need to try to act in better ways.

Contrition is only the first step we take. We want to show we are truly sorry and want to do better. And so we choose to prove this.

Doing Penance

This is what receiving a **penance** in the sacrament of Reconciliation is all about. The penance is an outward sign that you want to **repent,** or make up for any hurt you have caused. It is an outward sign that you want to change and to make better choices. The penance can even be a way to practice making better choices.

After you have confessed your sins to the priest, he will give you a penance to do. He may ask you to say several prayers, asking God to help you change the way you act. Sometimes, your penance may be to do something for someone who has been hurt by your actions. For example, if you have been fighting with your brother, the priest may ask you to spend some time playing with your brother peacefully, or helping with his chores. Or the priest may tell you to do one of the **Works of Mercy** as a penance. The Works of Mercy are ways that the followers of Jesus show they care for one another. You can find a list of these helping actions on page 78 of this book.

It is important to remember that penance is not magic. It doesn't make a person never do wrong again. Real change, real conversion, is a life-long process. It takes time and continual work.

Always Growing

Conversion means growing to be as much like Jesus as we can. That's a big responsibility. But we're not alone.

We have the Ten Commandments, the Great Commandment, and the example of Jesus to follow. We have the sacraments to give us strength. And we have the other members of God's Family to help us.

We also have **prayer.** Whenever and wherever we wish, we can talk to God, knowing that God listens and will give us what we need to grow and change.

We Catholics Believe

Conversion is making a change for the better in the way you think, choose, and act. Conversion is turning toward God's love and forgiveness.

Penance is something you agree to do to show that you are willing to make peace and to change your life. It is also a step in Reconciliation.

To **repent** is to feel sorry for your sins and to want to change to be better.

The **Works of Mercy** are actions that serve others physically or spiritually.

Prayer is words or actions that share our love for God. Four kinds of prayer are praise, thanksgiving, petition, and sorrow for sin. We can also pray to Mary and the saints.

The Woman Who Changed

Once, Jesus was invited to have supper with one of the teachers of the Law. Just as they were getting ready to eat, a woman pushed her way into the room. She was carrying a jar of perfumed ointment.

The woman threw herself down in front of Jesus and began to weep. She washed His feet with her tears, and dried them with her long hair. She poured the precious ointment on Jesus' feet. Then, she knelt quietly.

Simon, the teacher, was outraged. He recognized the woman. The whole town knew her as a sinner. Surely, if Jesus knew anything at all, Simon thought to himself, He would not let this bad woman touch Him!

Jesus knew what Simon was thinking. "Don't be so quick to condemn this woman," Jesus told Simon. "She has shown by her love and care for Me that she is sorry for her past and is trying to change her life. Simon, that is the best sign of reconciliation: love."

Jesus turned to the woman. "Your sins are forgiven," He told her gently. "Go now, and live in peace."

(based on Luke 7:36–50)

Thinking about Scripture

- How could Jesus tell that the woman was willing to change her life?

Choosing to Change

Imagine that the sentences below describe you and a choice you made. For each, write an action you could do that shows you want to do better.

1. The last time you went to the grocery store, you put some gum in your pocket without paying for it.

   You can pay for the gum.

2. Along with everyone else, you've ignored the new girl in class.

   You could pay attention to the new girl.

3. Math is confusing, so you count on Tony to give you homework answers.

   You can do your homework on your own.

4. You blamed your younger brother for doing something you actually did.

   You can tell you did the thing.

5. Everyone teases Beth, so you do, too.

   You can play with Beth.

6. Your Grandma calls you on the phone every Sunday, but you never feel like talking to her.

   Talk to your Grandma

Vocabulary

Write your own definitions for the following words: *talking to God and listening*

Prayer *a type of poem. Some written prayers can be poems*

Penance *a sacrament to bring you closer to God.*

Celebrating Forgiveness

Leader: Let us gather together in the name of the Father, and of the Son, and of the Holy Spirit.

All: Amen.

Leader: We are here to ask for God's forgiveness for the wrong choices we've made and the times we have turned away from God's love.

Reader 1: Lord, there have been times when we have refused to forgive someone. We didn't even forgive when they wanted us to. We're sorry.

All: Lord, have mercy. Kyrie eleison.

Reader 2: Lord, sometimes we have told people we have forgiven them. But, we didn't let go of our anger or hurt. We're sorry.

All: Christ, have mercy. Christe eleison.

Reader 3: Lord, sometimes we have gotten back at someone who has hurt us. We're sorry.

All: Lord, have mercy. Kyrie eleison.

Leader: We end with this prayer:

All: Lord, we are sorry for all our sins. We want to be like You—understanding and forgiving. Because we are forgiven by You, help us to be generous in forgiving others. Let our actions speak for our sorrow. Amen.

Family Note: Lesson 6 reminds us that contrition is not enough to make up for a wrong doing. Proof, or the desire for conversion, is needed. In Reconciliation, this proof is in the form of a penance. You can guide your child to practice conversion at home. When an action calls for forgiveness, help your child go beyond saying "I'm sorry" and actually do something that shows remorse. For example, if a younger brother was teased, the older child can offer to spend some one-on-one time with the brother. In the prayer service, Kyrie eleison and Christe eleison are Latin for Lord have mercy and Christ have mercy.

I Am Forgiven

Absolution

Priest: God, the Father of mercies, through the death and resurrection of His Son, has reconciled the world to Himself and sent the Holy Spirit among us for the forgiveness of sins; through the ministry of the Church may God give you pardon and peace. I absolve you from your sins in the name of the Father, and of the Son, and of the Holy Spirit.

Penitent: Amen.

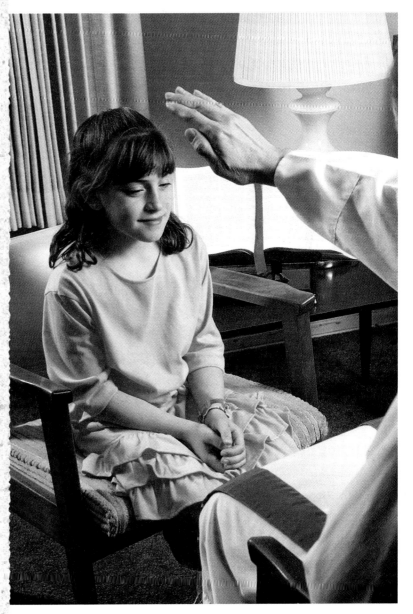

Healing

Every day after school, Amy took her dog, King, for a walk. Actually it was more of a run. Amy would ride her bike, and King would run along beside her.

This afternoon, Amy was very excited. For her birthday, her grandfather had given her an antique watch with a moon dial. Amy loved the watch. She kept glancing at it as she rode.

All of a sudden, King saw a cat. In chasing after it, he ran right in front of Amy's bike. Amy slammed on the brakes, but lost her balance. She toppled over onto the concrete.

Amy groaned as she felt a sharp pain in her left arm. She was almost afraid to look. Moving hurt so much! But Amy didn't really start to cry until she saw the pieces of her antique watch scattered all over the street.

Amy's parents rushed her to the hospital where x-rays were taken. They showed a break in Amy's forearm. "To help the bone come together again in just the right way," the doctor said, "we're going to put your arm in a cast."

A Slow Process

At first, Amy enjoyed the attention the cast caused. But as the weeks went by, the cast became a real bother. She couldn't play volleyball or basketball. She had a hard time riding her bike. And, since she could never get the cast wet, Amy couldn't wash her arm.

"It itches," Amy complained to her mother, "and I can't even scratch it."

"You'll just have to be patient," her mother said. "Healing takes a long time."

Finally, the day came for the cast to come off. Amy's parents and her grandfather took her to the doctor's office. When the doctor sawed the cast open and broke it apart, Amy looked down at her arm and wiggled her fingers.

"How does it feel?" the doctor asked.

"The arm feels great!" Amy replied. "Now, everything's back the way it was."

"Not quite," Amy's grandfather remarked. "You still need this."

Amy looked at the watch he was buckling on her wrist. "Grandpa, my watch! But how did you...?"

"Your dad gathered up all the pieces," he explained. "I took them to a jeweler. It took almost as long to be fixed as your arm did to heal!"

Amy smiled. She raised her wrist to the light. The moon face on her watch seemed to be smiling back.

Thinking about the Story

- Why did Amy need patience after breaking her arm?

Becoming Whole Again

Reconciliation is a process that is much like healing a broken bone. In fact, the word reconcile means "to heal or to bring together again."

What does it mean to be healed? It is to be whole and well. It is a feeling that everything is the way it should be. Sometimes healing occurs physically, like the bone in Amy's arm. Healing can also be spiritual and help us to be the kind of person God wants us to be.

Amy's broken arm was an accident. Sin is something you choose on purpose. There is a way the effect of sin is similar to the effect of Amy's accident. Sin causes a kind of "break" in our relationship with God and with others. We need spiritual healing.

Signs of Healing

The **Gospels** tell us that Jesus often healed sick people, spiritually and physically. He did this to show God's mercy and love. Over and over again, Jesus explained that God is a loving Father. "God will not hand you a stone when you ask for bread. Likewise, He will not punish you when you ask for forgiveness" (*Matthew 7:9,11*).

Since the people found it hard to believe that God could be so merciful and forgiving, Jesus also told them many stories and parables about God. Jesus said that God is like the shepherd who searches after each lost sheep and brings it safely back to the pasture. God is like the father who gives a big party when his runaway son returns home at last.

God's Love

The sacrament of Reconciliation is a celebration of healing. In this sacrament, you take the time to mend your relationship with God. You make peace with others, and you make peace with yourself. When you say that you are sorry and need forgiveness, the priest gives you **absolution.** Your relationship with God and with other members of God's Family is whole once again. Healing has taken place.

56

There are three ways you can receive absolution in the sacrament of Reconciliation. You can receive this sacrament in a confessional, where you and the priest are separated by a screen. Or, you can confess your sins to the priest face-to-face. You can also attend a parish Reconciliation service that includes individual confession and absolution. Each of these ways restores you to God's grace. Each of these ways gives you the joy of being healed.

We Catholics Believe

The **Gospels** are the New Testament accounts of the life and teachings of Jesus. The word gospel means "good news." Jesus often use parables to teach about God's kingdom.

The word **absolution** means "to wash." After you have confessed your sins and prayed an Act of Contrition in the sacrament of Reconciliation, the priest prays a prayer of absolution as a sign that God has forgiven you.

The Lost Coin

Jesus told this story to His friends.

Once, there was a poor woman who had only ten coins. She kept these coins in a secret place in her house. She could not afford to lose any of them.

But one day, she discovered that one of the coins was missing. The woman was very upset!

She lit a lamp and swept the entire house. She looked under the bed and behind each chair.

Finally, she found the coin she had lost.

The woman was so happy, she called together all her friends and neighbors. "Rejoice with me," she told them, "because I have just found the coin that I lost."

Then, Jesus said to His friends: "In just the same way, I tell you, there will be rejoicing among the angels of God over one sinner who repents."

(based on Luke 15:8–10)

Thinking about Scripture

* How is the lost coin like a person who sins?
* How is the woman in the story like God?

Healing Solutions

In each of the following situations, sin has disturbed the peace of a relationship. Imagine that these choices were yours. Then, think of a way to heal each situation.

1. You didn't go home when you were supposed to.

   Healing Solution: *Do extra chores.*

2. You made fun of your younger brother and called him names.

   Healing Solution: *ask your brother to forgive you.*

3. You stole a book that belongs to the library.

   Healing Solution: *Give the book back.*

In this space, draw or write about how you feel when you are forgiven.

I feel glad the person forgave me and sorry for what I did.

Vocabulary

good

Write your own definitions for the following words:

Absolution *forgiveness*

Healing *Making better*

Have Mercy on Us

Leader: We gather together in the name of the Father, and of the Son, and of the Holy Spirit.

All: Amen.

Reader: Listen to this story of God's merciful love. (*Read Matthew 18:12-14.*)

Leader: Jesus, like the sheep, we want to be found by Your love when we are lost.

All: Have mercy on us, O God, in Your goodness.

Leader: Like the shepherd, we want to show others how to follow You.

All: Have mercy on us, O God, in Your goodness.

Leader: Let us pray the words of Psalm 51.

All: Wash away our sins, Lord, and let us hear the sounds of joy and gladness. Create in us clean hearts, and renew our spirits within us. We will teach everyone about Your love, and sinners will return to You. Have mercy on us, O God, in Your goodness. Amen.

Family Note: Lesson 7 explains the meaning of absolution in Reconciliation. Forgiveness is described as a spiritual healing that restores us to God's grace. You may wish to light a candle as a symbol of God's presence when saying the prayer on this page.

60

Forgiving Others

Praise and Dismissal

Priest: Give thanks to the Lord, for He is good.

Penitent: His mercy endures forever.

Priest: May the Passion of our Lord Jesus Christ, the intercession of the Blessed Virgin Mary and of all the saints, whatever good you do and suffering you endure, heal your sins, help you grow in holiness and reward you with eternal life.

Penitent: Amen.

Forgiving

Kevin and Kenny were twins, but they were very different. Kenny was good in sports but not in studies. Kevin was a good student, but he couldn't play baseball or basketball.

One day, their teacher announced an essay contest with a brand-new computer as the prize.

The boys spent an entire week on their papers. Kevin had no trouble at all. He knew how to express himself, and spelling came easy. But Kenny had a difficult time. He felt that he couldn't write anything that sounded right.

The night before the papers were due, Kenny found Kevin's essay and read it. It was really good. Then he got an idea. Carefully, he copied the paper in his own hand-writing and put his name on it. Then he put his pages underneath Kevin's title page. The next day, he handed in both sets.

The teacher liked Kevin's paper the best. Since Kenny's name was on it, he won the computer.

For a week, Kenny did nothing but play computer games. But soon, he got bored. He began to feel sorry that he had switched papers with his brother. Finally, Kenny told Kevin what he had done.

Kevin was more than angry. Kevin was furious. "I hate you!" he yelled. "I wish you weren't my brother!"

Making Up

For days, Kevin didn't speak to Kenny nor would he sit with Kenny at lunch time. If Kenny walked into a room, Kevin walked out. When the two boys went to bed in the room they shared, Kevin turned out his light without saying "Good night."

Kenny couldn't stand it any more. He went to the teacher and told her what he had done. He asked her to announce the real winner in class the next day. The teacher was disappointed in Kenny, but she could see that he was sorry.

Kenny raced home after school. He moved the computer to Kevin's side of the room. Then, he left a note on the computer screen.

"Kevin," he wrote, "I'm really sorry. I told our teacher what I did. I told Mom and Dad, too. But I need you to forgive me. I'd rather have a brother than a computer. How can I make it up to you? Your brother, Kenny."

When Kevin got home, he read the note, but he was still very angry. Then he began to think how quiet it was without Kenny to talk to. He thought about the good times they had. Kevin felt his anger melting away. He knew Kenny would feel bad enough when the class found out what he had done.

Kevin found Kenny in the yard. "Hey," he said. "There's only one way you can make up for what you did."

"How?" Kenny asked, sadly.

"You can teach me how to play computer basketball!" Kevin laughed.

Forgiving Is a Choice

When someone cheats you, when a friend acts selfishly, when a parent breaks a promise, you experience many feelings. You may feel hurt, or you may feel angry. Like Kevin, you may feel that you never want to trust that person again.

These feelings are not unusual. But it is important to remember that in these situations, if you are the one who is hurt, you decide how to respond. You can choose to be resentful and angry. Or you can choose to be merciful and forgiving.

We Are Called to Forgive

Members of God's Family know that forgiving others is one way to follow the example of Jesus. Even when He was dying on the cross, Jesus prayed for those who had hurt Him. "Father, forgive them for they do not know what they are doing" (*Luke 23:34*). Forgiving others is a way to say thank you for the love and mercy God has shown us. Because God has forgiven our sins, we have the grace and strength to forgive others.

Before He ascended into heaven, Jesus gave the **Apostles** a mission. He told them that He wanted them to be ministers of forgiveness. "Whose sins you forgive are forgiven them, and whose sins you retain are retained" (*John 20:23*). From this mission of Jesus, priests and bishops are called to an ordained **ministry**. They receive the power to give absolution in the sacrament of Reconciliation.

Following Jesus

Of course, not all of the followers of Jesus are ordained ministers. But they are all called to follow Jesus through a ministry of service to others.

Development: We Believe

Jesus gave us some guidelines for leading happy, forgiving, and serving lives. We call these the **Beatitudes,** because the word beatitude means "blessed" or "happy." You can find these words of Jesus on page 79 of this book.

Learning to forgive others is an important part of seeking true happiness. People who can forgive do not carry around the weight of their anger. They do not hold grudges. They are not always looking for ways to "get even." They are free to be happy.

When we live the Beatitudes, we grow in our ability to forgive others and to restore peace. Above all, we put serving others before everything else.

We Catholics Believe

The **Apostles** were special friends of Jesus sent by Him to carry on His work.

Ministry is another word for service. In the sacrament of Holy Orders, bishops, priests, and deacons are given special grace and strength to serve the Church as **ordained ministers.** All Christians are called by the sacrament of Baptism to use their gifts and talents to serve others.

The **Beatitudes** are eight short sayings that Jesus told the people in His Sermon on the Mount. They tell us how to live a happy life on earth that will bring us everlasting happiness in heaven.

Peace Be with You

Several days after Jesus died, the Apostles gathered together in a secret place. They locked the door because they were afraid that the people in Jerusalem might kill them, too.

The Apostles weren't happy. They felt guilty that they had run away when Jesus was arrested. They felt sad that most of them had not stayed by Jesus when He was on the cross.

Suddenly, Jesus came and stood among them. "Peace be with you," He said. "Do not be afraid. I am Jesus."

The Apostles touched Jesus. They knew that God had raised Him from the dead, just as He had promised.

"Peace be with you," Jesus said again. This time, the Apostles began to feel better. They knew that Jesus loved them even though they made mistakes. They knew that God would be with them always in the days to come.

"I want you to share this peace with others," Jesus said to them. "Go out to all people and tell them how much God loves them. Forgive others, and I will forgive them, too."

The Apostles did this. They told people that God wanted them to be His children. They baptized people and shared Eucharist with them. They forgave those who had sinned. They also taught people to be at peace with one another.

(based on John 20:19–23 and Acts 2:37–47)

Thinking about Scripture

- Why were the Apostles afraid when they saw Jesus?
- How did the Apostles share the peace of Christ with others?

Sacrament Review

Here's what a person preparing for Reconciliation has to say about the sacrament. Circle **Yes** for every correct statement and circle **No** for every incorrect statement.

1. "Reconciliation helps me make better choices and follow Jesus more closely." (Yes) No

2. "Before I receive Reconciliation, I say a penance." (Yes) No *act of contrition*

3. "The priest may tell others what he hears during confession." Yes (No)

4. "Some sins are accidents or mistakes." (Yes) (No)

5. "Absolution is a sign of God's loving forgiveness." (Yes) No

6. "I can receive Reconciliation only once a year." Yes (No)

7. "The priest takes the place of God." (Yes) (No)

8. "I can receive Reconciliation in a confessional or in a Reconciliation room." (Yes) No

In the space below, write one or two sentences about what the sacrament of Reconciliation means to you.

It means becoming closer to God and Jesus to me.

One way we experience the peace Jesus promised us is through the sacrament of Reconciliation. We want to share this peace with others. Here is the Franciscan prayer that asks for God's help to be peacemakers.

Lord,
Make me an instrument of Your peace;
Where there is hatred, let me plant love;
Where there is injury, pardon;
Where there is doubt, faith;
Where there is despair, hope;
Where there is darkness, light;
Where there is sadness, joy.
Grant that I may not so much seek to be
    comforted as to comfort;
To be understood as to understand;
To be loved as to love.
For it is in giving that we receive,
    it is in pardoning that we are pardoned,
    and it is in dying that we are born to eternal life.

Family Note: Lesson 8 tells us that Reconciliation challenges us to live more like Jesus. It also gives us grace to build peace and to forgive others. Try to use your everyday family situations to guide your child to be a peacemaker.

Absolution   A word that means "to wash." After you have confessed your sins and prayed an Act of Contrition in the sacrament of Reconciliation, the priest prays a prayer of absolution as a sign that God has forgiven you. (*page 57*)

Apostles   Twelve close friends and followers of Jesus who were sent by Him to work in His name. (*page 65*)

Baptism   This sacrament of initiation washes away sin, gives new life, and joins us to God's Family. (*page 9*)

Beatitudes   Short sayings that Jesus told the people in His Sermon on the Mount. The word beatitude means "blessed" or "happy." The Beatitudes tell us how to gain eternal happiness by living Jesus' Way. (*page 65*)

Blessed Trinity   Our name for one God who is Father, Son, and Holy Spirit. (*page 9*)

Catholic   A word meaning "for everyone." The members of the Catholic Church are baptized and follow the authority of the pope and the bishops. (*page 9*)

Community   A group of people who share something in common. A family is a community because the members are all related to one another. A school is a community because people go there to learn and to grow. A parish is a community because its members believe in and follow Jesus. (*page 41*)

Confession   The act of telling your sins to a priest in the sacrament of Reconciliation. To confess means "to tell honestly or to admit something about yourself." This word is sometimes used as another name for the sacrament of Reconciliation. (*page 33*)

Conscience   God's gift that helps us know right from wrong. (*page 25*)

Consequences   The effects of your choices or actions. Consequences can affect both you and other people. Responsible people think about the consequences of their actions before they act. (*page 33*)

Contrition   A feeling of sorrow for sin and the promise to do better. (*page 41*)

Conversion   Making a change for the better and turning toward God's love and forgiveness. (*page 49*)

Covenant   A solemn agreement. God's covenant with the Israelites was sacred and loving. God would be with them always; in return, they promised to follow the Ten Commandments. We continue to live this covenant. (*page 17*)

Disciple   Someone who believes in and follows Jesus. (*page 10*)

Forgiveness   The act of pardoning someone who hurt you. (*page 41*)

Free will   God's gift that allows us to choose to walk with Jesus or away from God. (*page 25*)

Glossary

Golden Rule "Do to others whatever you would have them do to you" (*Matthew 7:14*). (*page 41*)

Gospels The Good News that tells the life and teachings of Jesus. (*page 57*)

Grace A share in God's life and love. (*page 25*)

Great Commandment "You shall love the Lord, your God, with all your heart, with all your being, with all your strength, and with all your mind. And, you must love your neighbor as your-self" (*based on Matthew 22:34-40*). (*page 17*)

Heaven Being happy with God forever. (*page 65*)

Hell Total and lasting separation from God's love. (*page 33*)

Humility The ability to be honest about oneself. Humble people know both their good points and their bad points. They can admit when they are wrong. They have the courage to say "I am sorry." (*page 41*)

Israelites Another name for the Jewish people. They are called Israelites because they are the children of Jacob, whose name was also Israel. Moses led the Israelites out of slavery and into freedom. (*page 9*)

Jesus The Son of God and our Savior. (*page 10*)

Messiah The Savior; the person picked by God to help the people of Israel live the way God wanted them to live. Christians believe that Jesus is the Messiah. (*page 33*)

Ministry Another word for service. Bishops, priests, and deacons are ordained ministers. Through Baptism, all Christians are called to serve others. (*page 65*)

Original sin The first sin. Only Jesus and His Mother, Mary, were born without original sin. Jesus saved us from original sin, but its effects are still with us. (*page 25*)

Parable A special story used by Jesus to teach His Way. There are many parables in the four Gospels. (*page 26*)

Penance An action that is done in order to show sorrow and a willingness to change. Also, a step in Reconciliation. (*page 49*)

Penitent A person who is sorry for sinning. (*page 5*)

Prayer Words or actions that share our love for God. Four types of prayer are praise, thanksgiving, petition, and sorrow for sin. (*page 49*)

Reconciliation One of the seven sacraments of the Catholic Church. In this sacrament, a person confesses his or her sins to a priest, expresses sorrow for these sins, and promises to do better in the future. The priest forgives the person, in the name of God and the members of God's Family. (*page 9*)

Repent To feel sorry for sin; to change one's life. Jesus asked His followers to repent and to turn toward God. (*page 49*)

Responsible The ability to be answerable for the wrong choices that are made. (*page 33*)

Sacrament One of the special signs and celebrations of God's love. Jesus gave us seven sacraments: Baptism, Confirmation, Eucharist, Reconciliation, Anointing of the Sick, Marriage, and Holy Orders. These sacraments give God's own life, or grace, to the members of the Church. They help the members grow. (*page 9*)

Sin Choosing to do wrong. Venial sin hurts our friendship with God. Mortal sin ruins our friendship with God. Mortal sin is sometimes called deadly sin, because it separates us from grace, our share in God's life. (*page 25*)

Ten Commandments The laws God gave Moses on Mount Sinai. These ten laws told the Israelites how to live in peace and love. We follow these commandments today. (*page 17*)

Works of Mercy Actions that serve others physically and spiritually. (*page 49*)

Reconciliation

Important Things to Know about Reconciliation

Sin is turning away from God by choosing to do wrong. Sin is a failure to respond with love to God and to others.

- **Venial sin** is choosing something that is wrong that hurts our friendship with God. To receive forgiveness for venial sin, we must be sincerely sorry and ask God, in prayer, to help us live better lives.

- **Mortal sin** is choosing something that is very seriously wrong. A person who chooses mortal sin is choosing to turn away from God's love and from God's Family. Mortal sin is sometimes called deadly sin, because it separates us from grace, our share in God's life.

- For a sin to be mortal, the action must be seriously wrong. The person must know that the action is seriously wrong and chooses to commit the action anyway. No one can commit a mortal sin by mistake or by accident.

- To receive forgiveness for mortal sin, it is necessary to confess the sin to a priest in the sacrament of Reconciliation. The person must be sincerely sorry for the sin and willing to make up for the serious wrong he or she has done. This is shown through the performing of the penance given by the priest. The priest, taking the place of Jesus, says a prayer of absolution as a sign of God's forgiveness and of our reconciliation with God's Family.

Questions about the Sacrament of Reconciliation

1. **When should I receive the sacrament of Reconciliation for the first time?** Most young Catholics who were baptized as babies will receive the sacrament of Reconciliation for the first time at about the age of seven—when they are old enough to know the difference between right and wrong. Usually, you will receive the sacrament of Reconciliation for the first time just before you make your First Communion.

2. **How often should I receive the sacrament of Reconciliation?** Catholics are required to confess any mortal sin at least once a year, during the Easter season. Because you cannot receive Holy Communion while you are in a state of mortal sin, it is important to confess any serious sins as soon as possible. But Reconciliation is not just important in times of mortal sin. Regular, frequent confession of venial sin will help you overcome bad habits and bring you closer to God.

3. **What if I have committed a serious sin, and I cannot get to the sacrament of Reconciliation?** In a grave emergency (such as the danger of death), you can receive absolution from mortal sin by praying a sincere Act of Contrition and by promising God you will try to change your life. You should try to receive the sacrament of Reconciliation as soon as you possibly can.

4. **What if the priest is angry with me, or tells my sins to someone else?** In confession, the priest takes the place of Jesus. He is not there to judge you or to yell at you, but to offer you God's forgiveness. If you have difficulty talking to a particular priest, you may choose to make your confession to another priest. All priests are bound by a sacred promise to keep what they hear in confession private. Anything you say in confession remains a secret.

How to Go to Confession

Before Receiving the Sacrament

Spend some time quietly thinking about what you will confess. You can use the Examination of Conscience on page 75 of this book to see how you are living the commandments.

Say a prayer to the Holy Spirit. Ask the Holy Spirit to help you make a good confession.

Wait quietly until it is your turn to enter the Reconciliation room or confessional. Be courteous to others who are waiting.

Steps in the Sacrament of Reconciliation
(Individual)

1. The priest greets you in the name of the Father, and of the Son, and of the Holy Spirit.

2. The priest says a prayer to help you trust in God. You answer, "Amen."

3. The priest may read a passage from Scripture to remind you of God's love and forgiveness. You listen quietly.

4. You tell your sins to the priest. Then, he talks with you about how you might make better choices.

5. The priest gives you a penance—something you agree to do in order to make up for your sins and to show that you want to change your life.

6. The priest invites you to tell God how sorry you are. You pray an Act of Contrition.

7. The priest prays the prayer of absolution. If you are making your confession face-to-face, the priest will extend his hands over your head while he prays. You say, "Amen."

8. The priest prays: "Give thanks to the Lord, for He is good." You answer, "His mercy endures forever."

9. The priest says, "The Lord has freed you from your sins. Go in peace."

Reconciliation

(*With a Group*)

1. The Reconciliation service may begin with a hymn. The priest greets the penitents and prays the Opening Prayer. You respond, "Amen."

2. Listen to the Scripture readings.

3. Listen to the homily.

4. Participate in the Examination of Conscience, which may be silent or in the form of a litany.

5. Pray the Act of Contrition or Litany of Sorrow, followed by the Lord's Prayer.

6. Confess and receive absolution individually.

7. Gather again to sing or pray in thanksgiving for God's mercy.

8. The priest says the concluding prayer. You respond, "Amen."

9. The priest blesses all present in the name of the Father, and of the Son, and of the Holy Spirit.

10. The priest or deacon dismisses the assembly by saying, "The Lord has freed you from your sins. Go in peace." You respond, "Amen."

After Receiving the Sacrament

- Remain in the church for a few moments. Say a prayer of thanksgiving to Jesus for the grace and healing you have received.

- If the priest has asked you to say prayers as your penance, you may pray these prayers quietly now. If the priest has asked you to do something as your penance, plan how you can carry out this action soon.

- Do not talk with others about your confession. Do not ask others about their confessions.

An Examination of Conscience

You can use these questions to prepare for the sacrament of Reconciliation. The questions are based on the Ten Commandments.

1. Do I really love God above all other things?
Do I put God first in my life?
Do I trust in God's love for me?
Do I avoid relying on supersition or "magic"?

2. Do I show respect for God's name?
When I make promises, do I take them seriously?
Do I show reverence for holy people, places, and things?
Is my language respectful and clean?

3. Do I participate fully at Mass?
Am I a part of my parish family?
Do I take time for prayer and spiritual growth?
How do I use my leisure time?

4. Do I contribute to my family's happiness?
Am I obedient to my parents and others in authority?
Do I show love for my brothers and sisters?
How well do I show repect for older adults?

5. Do I respect God's gift of life?
Do I take care of my health and the well-being of others?
Am I able to avoid the temptation to use drugs or alcohol?

Do I avoid violence and fighting in my life and in what I watch or read?

6. Do I show respect for the human body and for God's gift of sexuality?
Do I avoid situations, entertainments, and conversations that make fun of God's gift of sexuality?
Am I modest and chaste in my thoughts, my words, and my actions?

7. Do I avoid cheating and stealing?
Do I take care of my possessions and respect the belongings of others?
Am I careful to make sure that others get their fair share?

8. Am I honest with others and with myself?
Can people put their trust in me?
Do I avoid lying?
Do I refuse to gossip about others or call them names?

9. Do I show respect for marriage and family life?
Do I recognize that responsible sexuality requires the mature commitment of marriage?
Am I jealous of my friends, or can I be open to new relationships and allow others that freedom, too?

10. Am I happy with what I have, or am I always asking for more?
Do I run others down out of envy? Do I let material possessions run my life?
Do I do my part in caring for God's creation?

Music

We Are a Kingdom People

Words and music by Christopher Walker

We are a kingdom people, kingdom people
Sent to love and serve our God.
We are a kingdom people, a kingdom
people sent to love and serve our God.

1. We serve Jesus ev'ry time we help our
   brothers and sisters, brothers and sisters.

2. We serve Jesus ev'ry time we share the
   good things God gives us, good things
   God gives us.

3. We serve Jesus ev'ry time that we are
   honest and truthful, honest and truthful.

Choices

Words by Cathy Ruff
Music by David Phillips

I am learning to make choices, and now's
   the time to start
To listen and obey God's rule, the choice is
   in my heart.
I am learning to make choices, and now's
   the time to start
To listen and obey God's rule, the choice is
   in my heart.

1. There's always rules to follow, at home,
     at play.
   God knew I'd need a helping hand each
     and ev'ry day.
   So God gave us commandments,
     rules we must obey.

2. Gossiping and lying cause destruction
     and despair,
   But honesty and words of praise show
     others that we care.
   If somehow you have hurt someone,
     don't think the pain will hide.

Your Way, O God

Words and music by Bob Hurd

Your way, O God, I want to follow,
Help me to walk the path of life.
You are the Shepherd, we are the sheep,
Teach us the sound of Your voice.

1. Help us to make this journey together,
   Help us to share the Bread of Life.
   We must be Christ for each other
   For we are Your own.

2. Sometimes we hurt ourselves
   And each other,
   And we feel lost, ashamed and alone.
   You sent us Jesus to find us
   And lead us home.

More Joy in Heaven

Words and music by Marie Jo Thum

. There once was a shepherd who loved
all his sheep.
They numbered on hundred fold,
But one little lamb wandered away,
Was frightened and lonely and cold.
With ninety-nine safe in the field
The shepherd set out to rescue his stray
And when he returned with his lamb in
his arms
He invited his neighbors to stay. He said,

(Refrain)
Come, share my happiness,
Feast at my table.
Join me with great jubilation.
Do you not know what was lost has been
found?

Rejoice in my glad celebration!
And there is more joy in heaven,
There is more joy in heaven,
There is more joy in heaven,
There is more joy in heaven
When the lost one has returned.

2. There once was a father who loved
both his sons,
But his younger son wanted to roam.
He squandered their money
and lived like a fool
And sadly he started for home.
Sorry and shameful he cried to his father,
"Your servant," he said. "Let me be."

But his father embraced him and said,
"You're my son,
and my son you'll
Always be."
He said, (*Sing the refrain.*)

Oh, Happy One

Words and music by Marie Jo Thum

Oh, happy one! Come and rejoice!
The kingdom of heaven belongs to you!
Oh, happy one! Come and rejoice!
The kingdom of heaven belongs to you,
Oh happy one!

1. God is your treasure, God knows all
your needs.
Blest are the poor in spirit.
Look for the good in ev'rything and
ev'ryone.
Blest are the clean of heart.

2. Say yes to God. Accept God's will with
courage.
Blessed are the meek.
Treat other people as you want them to
treat you.
Blest are those who hunger for justice.

3. Do the right thing, even when it is
not easy.
Blest are those who suffer in My name.
Give up power and instead bring peace.
Blessed are those who bring peace.

4. Show God's mercy. Be kind and
forgiving.
Blest are the merciful.
Suffer with those who hurt
And share their tears.
Blessed are those who mourn.

Prayers

The Sign of the Cross

In the name of the Father,
  and of the Son,
  and of the Holy Spirit.
Amen

The Lord's Prayer

Our Father, who art in heaven,
  hallowed be Thy name.
Thy kingdom come; Thy will be done
  on earth as it is in heaven.
Give us this day our daily bread,
  and forgive us our trespasses
  as we forgive those who trespass
  against us.
And lead us not into temptation
  but deliver us from evil.
Amen.

The Hail Mary

Hail, Mary, full of grace,
  the Lord is with thee.
Blessed art thou among women,
  and blessed is the Fruit
  of thy womb, Jesus.
Holy Mary, Mother of God,
  pray for us sinners, now,
  and at the hour of our death.
Amen.

Glory to the Father

Glory to the Father,
  and to the Son.
  and to the Holy Spirit.
As is was in the beginning,
  is now, and will be forever.
Amen.

Acts of Contrition

My God, I am sorry for my sins with all
  my heart.
In choosing to do wrong and failing to do
  good,
I have sinned against You
  whom I should love above all things.
I firmly intend, with Your help,
  to do penance, to sin no more,
  and to avoid whatever leads me to sin.
Jesus Christ suffered and died for us.
In His name, dear Father, forgive me.
Amen.

O my God,
I am heartily sorry for having offended
  Thee.
And I detest all my sins,
  because of Thy just punishments,
  but most of all because they offend
  Thee, my God,
  who art all good and deserving of all
  my love.
I firmly resolve, with the help of Thy grace,
  to sin no more,
  and to avoid the near occasion of sin.
Amen.

Lord, Jesus Christ, Son of God,
  have mercy on me, a sinner.

The Ten Commandments
(*based on Exodus 20:2–17*)

1. I am the Lord, your God. You shall have no other gods besides Me.
2. You shall not take the name of the Lord, your God, in vain.
3. Remember to keep holy the Sabbath day.
4. Honor your father and your mother.
5. You shall not kill.
6. You shall not commit adultery.
7. You shall not steal.
8. You shall not lie.
9. You shall not desire your neighbor's wife.
10. You shall not desire anything that belongs to your neighbor.

The Rules of the Church

1. Take part in the Eucharist every Sunday and holy day. Do no unnecessary work on Sunday.
2. Receive the sacraments frequently.
3. Study about the Good News of Jesus Christ.
4. Follow the marriage laws of the Church.
5. Support the people of God.
6. Do penance on certain days.
7. Reach out to other people. Support the missionary effort of the Church.

The Works of Mercy
Corporal (*For the Body*)
Feed the hungry.
Give drink to the thirsty.
Clothe the naked.
Shelter the homeless.
Visit the sick.
Visit the imprisoned.
Bury the dead.

Spiritual (*For the heart, soul, and mind*)
Help the sinner.
Teach the ignorant.
Counsel the doubtful.
Comfort the sorrowful.
Bear wrongs patiently.
Forgive injuries.
Pray for the living and the dead.

The Beatitudes
(*based on Matthew 5:3–10*)
Blessed are the poor in spirit,
for theirs is the kingdom of heaven.
Blessed are they who mourn,
for they will be comforted.
Blessed are the meek,
for they will inherit the land.
Blessed are they who hunger and thirst for righteousness,
for they will be satisfied.
Blessed are the merciful,
for they will be shown mercy.
Blessed are the clean of heart,
for they will see God.
Blessed are the peacemakers,
for they will be called children of God.
Blessed are they who are persecuted for the sake of righteousness,
for theirs is the kingdom of heaven.

Lists Catholics Remember

The Seven Sacraments

Sacraments of Initiation
    Baptism
    Confirmation
    Eucharist
Sacraments of Healing
    Reconciliation
    The Anointing of the Sick
Sacraments of Service
    Marriage
    Holy Orders

The Gifts of the Holy Spirit
(from the Rite of Confirmation)

Wisdom	Knowledge
Understanding	Reverence
Right judgment	Wonder and awe
Courage	

The Fruit of the Spirit
(from Galatians 5:22–23)

Love	Generosity
Joy	Faithfulness
Peace	Gentleness
Patience	Self-control
Kindness	

The Virtues

Theological Virtues
    Faith
    Hope
    Love
Cardinal Virtues
    Prudence
    Justice
    Temperance
    Fortitude

Days of Penance

The days of Advent
Ash Wednesday
The days of Lent, specially Fridays
Fridays throughout the year